More Than, Less Than

Joanne Mattern

ROURKE PUBLISHING

www.rourkepublishing.com

www.rourkepublishing.com

PHOTO CREDITS: Cover: © PeskyMonkey; Title Page: © MaszaS; Page 3: © Tina Rencely; Page 5: © hkuchera, © AbbieImages; Page 7: © Craig Vetri, © James Trice; Page 9, 11: © parkhomenko, © Tihis; Page 13, 15: © Don Nichols; Page 17, 19: © carlosalvarezl Page 21, 23: © PhotoEuphoria, © Mixmike

Edited by Kelli L. Hicks

Cover and Interior design by Tara Raymo

Library of Congress Cataloging-in-Publication Data

Mattern, Joanne, 1963-
 More than, less than / Joanne Mattern.
   p. cm. -- (Little world math concepts)
 Includes bibliographical references and index.
 ISBN 978-1-61590-291-0 (Hard Cover) (alk. paper)
 ISBN 978-1-61590-530-0 (Soft Cover)
 1. Number concept--Juvenile literature. I. Title.
 QA141.15.M28 2011
 513.2--dc22
                        2010009891

Rourke Publishing
Printed in the United States of America, North Mankato, Minnesota
020111
01312011LP-A

ROURKE
PUBLISHING

www.rourkepublishing.com - rourke@rourkepublishing.com
Post Office Box 643328 Vero Beach, Florida 32964

Some numbers are more than other numbers. Some numbers are less than other numbers. What's the difference?

The group of grapes is more than the group of raisins.

More ➜

Less ➜

The group of balls is less than the group of jacks.

More ➜

Less ➜

Which group of vegetables has more than the other?

There are more carrots than peas.
Six is more than four.

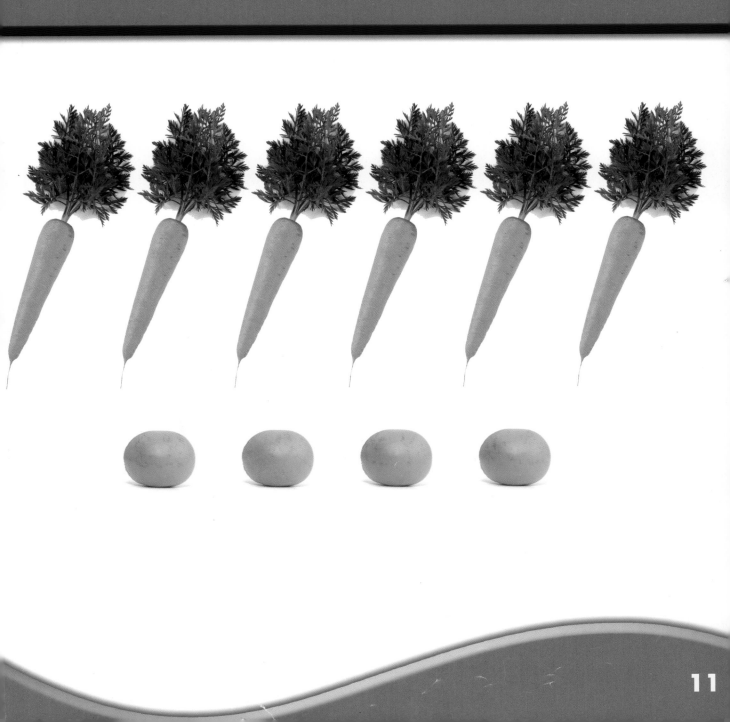

Which group of pencils has more than the other?

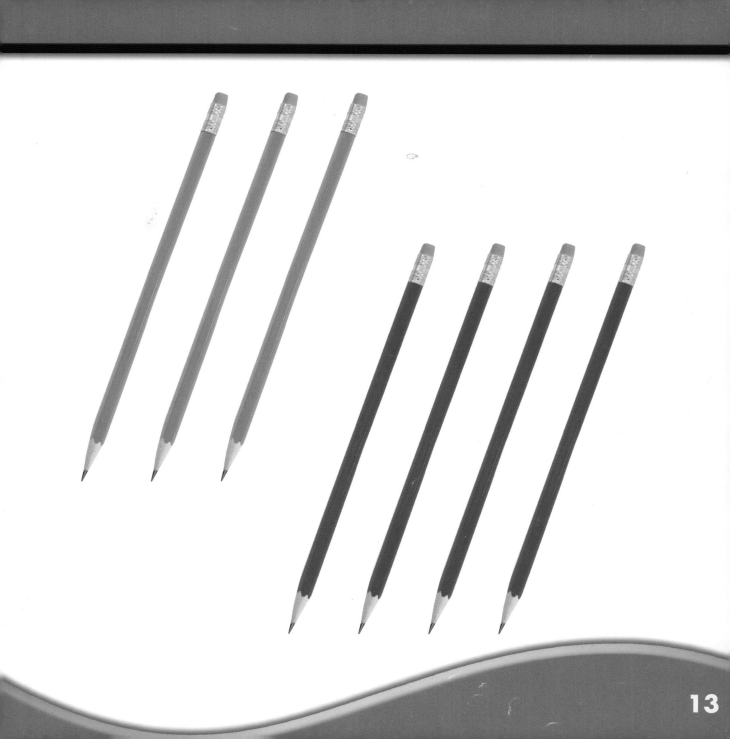

13

There are more blue pencils than red pencils. Four is more than three.

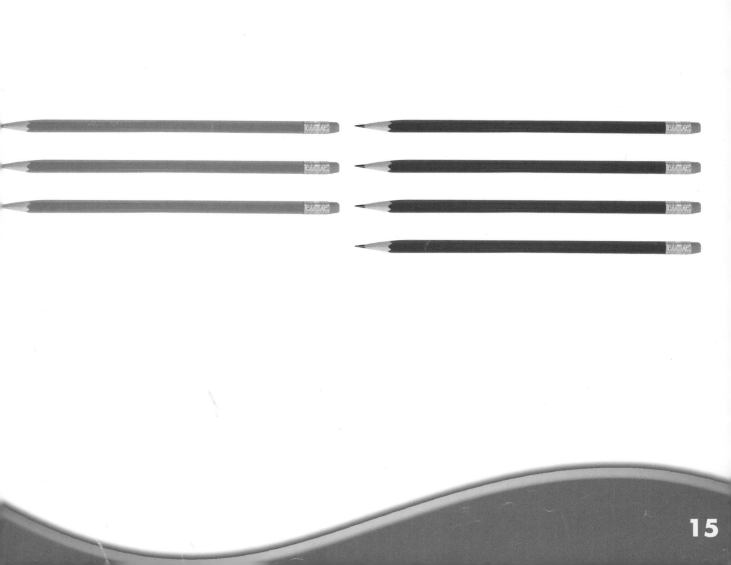

Which group has fewer blocks?

There are fewer green blocks than red blocks. Two is less than five.

Which group has fewer pieces
of candy?

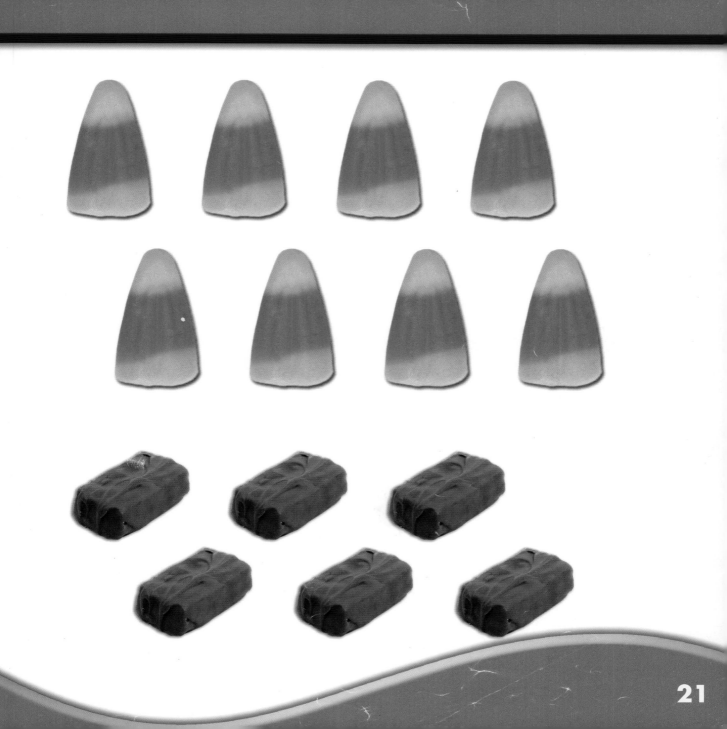

There are fewer pieces of chocolate.
Six is less than eight.

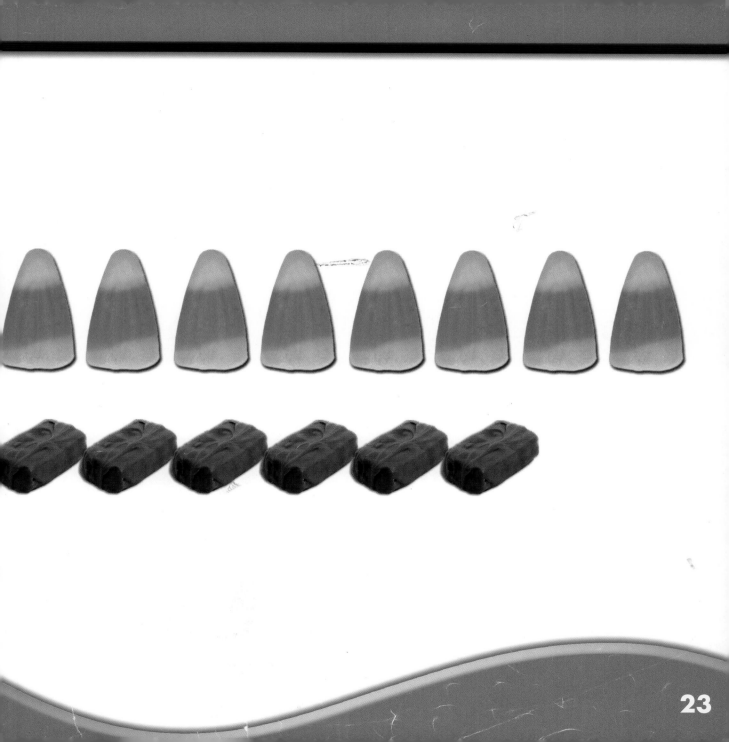

Index

Websites

www.songsforteaching.com/jennyfixmanedtunes/alligatorgreaterlessthan.htm

www.abcya.com/counting_fish.html

education.com/worksheet/article/less-or-more-than/

About the Author

Joanne Mattern has written more than 300 books. She lives in New York State with her husband, four children, and an assortment of pets that includes less than 4 cats, more than 1 gecko, more than 1 fish, and less than 2 turtles.